THE SHOES OF THE FISHERMAN'S WIFE

Praise for *The Shoes of the Fisherman's Wife: Poems*

"This is the poet as truth sayer—a long poetic interlude between a jazz break, steeped in fable, allegory, and magical realism. This collection's foundation is a Black radical tradition that pays homage to those who made American art in vogue: the runaways, the fugitives, the ones who were never allowed to capture the spirit of Western civilization. If I were a judge on a panel, I would fight for it to be awarded the prize every time."—Randall Horton, author of the American Book Award–winning *{#289-128}: Poems*

"upfromsumdirt writes of his life as a Black boy and man; of how he has lived that life sometimes as ghost, other times as animal, not always as human; of his love for his partner and the tiny, intricate beauties of the earth and human connection; of poetry as the landscape of radical liberatory imagination. His use of English against itself—combined with his ironic, irreverent, yet deeply sincere and vulnerable tone—feels propulsive and prescient. This is a much-needed entry into the literary conversation at large."—Ariana Benson, author of the Cave Canem Prize–winning *Black Pastoral: Poems*

"Sonically resplendent and agile af (as foretold; chronologically, thematically, geographically), upfromsumdirt once again astounds us with vibrant songs in his particular vein of Black vernacular poetry. Rife with love songs, account-giving, myth-tracing, and critiques of American institutions (also the self-as-poet), this collection brings readers to the gleaming edges of language." —Han VanderHart, author of *Larks: Poems* and host of the *Of Poetry Podcast*

"Splitting vernaculars from archaic to gutter, upfromsumdirt's journey as poet/griot/tragic hero continues dazzlingly. Rising from Kentucky hills and kitchens, new mythologies are fused from old, primordially Black. Our digital world is here, yet rooted in natural magic, woven with odes to a bountiful love that's home. Vulgar wit sparks flame."—Chantal James, author of *None but the Righteous: A Novel*

"Among visions that combine a past, both mythical and ancestral, with a future of gods and science fiction, there are present moments of beautiful tendernesses. Each page, each poem, is solid and powerful. *The Shoes of the Fisherman's Wife* delivers a truly exciting read."—David Harrison Horton, author of *Necessary* and *Model Answers*

THE SHOES OF THE FISHERMAN'S WIFE

POEMS

UPFROMSUMDIRT

UNIVERSITY PRESS OF KENTUCKY

Published by the University Press of Kentucky

Scholarly publisher for the Commonwealth, serving Bellarmine University, Berea College, Centre College of Kentucky, Eastern Kentucky University, The Filson Historical Society, Georgetown College, Kentucky Historical Society, Kentucky State University, Morehead State University, Murray State University, Northern Kentucky University, Simmons College, Spalding University, Transylvania University, University of Kentucky, University of Louisville, University of Pikeville, and Western Kentucky University.

Editorial and Sales Offices: The University Press of Kentucky
663 South Limestone, Lexington, Kentucky 40508-4008
www.kentuckypress.com

"Chiaroscuro Vita" and "What Light through *Beyond* Yonder Window" previously appeared, in slightly different form, in *slips slips* literary journal.

Cataloging-in-Publication data available from the Library of Congress

ISBN 978-1-9859-0345-6 (hardcover)
ISBN 978-1-9859-0346-3 (paperback)
ISBN 978-1-9859-0348-7 (pdf)
ISBN 978-1-9859-0347-0 (epub)

ASSOCIATION of UNIVERSITY PRESSES

Member of the Association of University Presses

in memory of

Once upon a Time in the Projects
—the Roanoke Colony of Internet Poetry Message Boards

that 2 and 2 are 5
that the forest miaows
that the tree plucks the maroons from the fire
that the sky strokes its beard
etc. etc. . . .

—AIMÉ CÉSAIRE,
NOTEBOOK OF A RETURN TO THE NATIVE LAND

Contents

THE STORY THUS FAR

Black Vernacular
fruit-bearing tho ~~frostbitten~~ freezer-burnt
in shared ilium.

BAS-RELIEF 1

write of glaciered moon
while yet, beneath the sternum:
i am pablum of sun

. . .

LAY PRONE

clinging as if black mold
as in the laundry room behind the chifforobe
or like Khepera the Greathearted

turned gentle cockchafer & rendered isabelline
incised to yield to tempestuous longing's
fleck desire for *Forever More*'s

    everlasting song
            and we are rife with it
—this tumultuous black mold;

its utter tempestuousity
that terribly clings to
the alluvia of Black Love:

the celestial mortar that binds us all;
the tenebrous silhouette to which
every star above is clung & made alight

our spiritual detritus deemed a Black supernal
like some sepia-cheeked tub-thumping cherub
come to herald the returning sun—

the exquisite held in contempt
until it propagates *the quaint,*
if not every day then every other day.

FAGAN'S GAMBOL

for Billie Holiday

The lawn is not yet brash enough
Its seasonal brass in slow surrender
Its verdant onset preening
This peacocking earth—*O, Comely Ingénue*
    O, Sacrosanct Jazz Beldam
With sun un-hocked from boondock and
Sky's overturned grey spewing in vigorous filigree:

    Our bronze garniture in festive donnybrook
    'Til winter's misconstrued villainy lays broken
    & by way of Eleanora, anchored in hither's renewal
    Gilded by every appliqué of springing yawn—
    After harvest / awaiting yield   *Carcel'd*
    By each gardenia to April's prodigious dawn.

This thrushing, fertile throng—
As if Sunday, as if phenomenal clay sewn in song.

JFKDLS;A (ORISON TO THE ORISHAS)

may I decompose in private wherever I am found dead
forgive me if I deceased at a breakfast table like mama's
daddy or was it daddy's daddy worn down gone to rot like
the old crease in a pleather couch feet up watching Netflix
with bowls of Cheetos over-strewn the dust particles
leaving my soul as if parading stars in mild procession
I mean I mean no mere inconvenience I just want my bones
to be a beacon caked in earth Pompeii-like by mounds of love
& capitalist debt pickled in amber & useless apps before found
ten centuries later graciously cocooned in my natural state
in boxers playing Wordle on a cell phone "in my spot" on the couch
—another romantically wild artifact of mythic African American
cataclysm my ruins the cardinal fixture spotlit under curio
as effulgently black as a monophone highboy heavier than
the first Remington QWERTY *upfromsumdirt* a Prime Meridian
an Optical Abrasion an Octavian Poet Vending Machine on
lisinopril & nighttime oxygen with congested poems & inflamed
knees might I be *a sigh for sore eyes;* may I close my screens
pillow head shutter focus & binge myself in radiant theme.

CHIAROSCURO VITA

—an artist's statement

Reedian
I contemplate LaBas then walk
the dark streets in flightless pidgin
errands in my pockets pennies taped
over eyelids in palladium / agate-brained
—I fake it to the stage
my inner thoughts cirrusly doused
my wandering I (everywhere) fermenting &
                                                                houseless

"I might be insane," says the early-onset dementia . . .
or at least tormented
    another tortured artist for Egun's sake!
if not *insane* sad.
tremendously sad. *the one who wheres the ask*
{raucous laughter ensues}—mask-plastered . . .
                                                                rouseless

not sad   *clinically disquiet*
(boo hue?   *hue's gonna check me*)
            it's not easy being glean

my hand alight fondles a heron's bone—neckless
{caucus laughter pursues} *the artist as rupture of a portrait*
every page fecklessly deckled a pack of fractured pixels a Bic pic
a splatch an ink splotch a hopscotching black batching blotch
poems travel gallimaufry through pastiche towards Rorschach

(booty-scratching back-scratching
turntable-scratching cornea-scra—)

but then *ta-dah!* coronal mass reflection

I tare my clothes beneath the sun—I'm pared
by its light • I stare into its bathos / my soul
stairing into the night • I altar my cites until
my sealings collapse & I dare to rite
what all is scene.

"SOMETIMES IT SNOWS IN . . . " *(WELL, YOU KNOW THE REST)*

Crystal's grandfather
our granddaughter and a grandson
—all born on April 9th

my father too in April tho later
so I'm very familiar with *the verdant*

I don't fear the verdant
and neither, too, am I afraid of *hither* in poetry
—you see, the old black persona comes pleated with earth

so, who am I if not the rain?
at once welcoming &

un-welcomed.

WHAT LIGHT THROUGH *BEYOND* YONDER WINDOW

& if you must know—
the worn & beleaguered merman
fills his deep atlantic pockets to the brim
with the heads of benthic seahorses
& the heady poems of mythic black folk both
floating to surface in ambush of sky
& if you wish to know—
i open mouth and wallow you
you swollen fish hallow in my navel
i scale the gleam in your eyes,
my medulla gasping for reflective rapture
until (in all the underwater caves of verse)
            ((pocketing a disassembled sun))
the horizon gently surrenders furl, the milium
of morning sun—its vicious onslaught of curious dawn;
our united ilia flaring towards chorale
until the ocean between us is indiscernible
our conjoined niche devoid of crestfallen sorrow
: a *drawning*   :: an *undrowning*
my heart, bloated from your smile;
muffled by your light—this, tho, *tbh,*
we both know you already know & yet you marvel
as to why i'm emotionally concussed my corneas reshaped
to your fictitious cameo my heart bending to your grace
filters your shadow & that i am visibly wracked should

go without question as your refusal
to laud me with decisive vow canonically vexes
but, shrew, it was your house demanding
in excessive dowry i build you this balcony
—don't vacate now your avouchment to leap!
you saw my stygian tongue and assumed
it meant *bawd* when it said *bard* so now refuses
to bow & construe a lyric for thine own comfort
(therefore when i clepe there is no wherefore)
& since you refuse to know—
my anachronisms bear a raft, neither sundeck nor rift
—my oceanic timbres swaling through umbras
rising through haptic dark—*but, soft!* (not soft.)

BAS-RELIEF 2

i kneel at you
grateful for your runnels.
my blood
in graceful burgeoning,
a fountain of mountains

aether/ore

. . .

DWELL LIKE A GHOST

fingertips
like daffodils in sweltering residency at the edge of palm,
a dust storm across the rusty creases where I'm the most
Augean

your touch
a besom sweeping across a calliope of ribs or as a swarm
of purple martins huffing melanin in leisure / the luminous swallow
making roost against zestful skin

sparking daylight
inside delighted growl, the hunger rising to crest, to dwell
like ghosts within the crusts
between us.

POETRY, ITS PELT

it's dead / i
should skin it
the blade tip—point blank
& attack ready
our carcass
of language
hung on shrapnel
of drying spit;
the cured tongue
a salted ham.

american poetry
is a white pride aspic
served as entitlement
to the desiccated reserves
of poor black piety;
its sleight vitality
fills our coffers.

i dig my bill
into its brain
& varied entrails;
deconstruct its veins
into sanctuary.

oh, my literary elephant-bird,
your inanimate growl
lines my ledgers;
i tuft my crown
in your sorrows.

I'M NOT AFRAID IN THESE WOODS

with their frail gaunt branches
high above slender stalks of pine

brown scritch scratches of skeletal limbs outstretched
the wooded skyscraper an unsteady walker reaching up

for mother's hem reaching out against disconsolate sky
these woods like a silhouette of quivers nestled in a missile launcher

i look in wonder to this nappy canopy beneath the empyreal / divine
thwarter of all thrown ropes / this sallow arboretum

arising in the dusk: this prim, poplar, quantum cadaver
(all things considered)—is almost an equalizer

if only   my wrists were free & feet untied . . .
    [my laughter lashes out in the gloomtide]

::

as oft, blood-pollen—
our brawn topocentric tongue
b'reft of dew   . . . or dawn.

DON QUIXOTE DEI

how offensive to you they are: with their non-white
windmills shepherding gales regarding privilege

with their solar panes collecting infernal glare
how communist / it's just wires & sheets of glass

said a sunless man raised on Helios praising
his own pathological pantheon beneath

his skins of cotton / flat berthing the entire world:
suspend, he says, *with your diverse perversity!*

their populism of Golden Calves; a wild-eyed
prohibition for the lachrymose woebegone

—Social Studies and Human History denied
real legion within Chris Rufo's Septic Crusade.

MANSA MUSA DISCOVERS *THE OLD WORLD* & NAMES IT LITTLE AFRICA

i'm grand sommelier of all the shadows
& my Wadjet always watches.
said: croon me and i surface;
huff and puff and i appear.
Brother Khepra keeps all my secrets;
Albert Ayler tracks the score.
—PRESTER JOHN SPEAKING FOR MANSA MUSA AS
RELAYED TO MANUEL I KOMNENOS (PROBABLY)

never again shall we address each other
without canonical consecration

haberdashers, we are, for a celestial undergrowth
receptionists for our Egungun this spoken spindle

with no bits or bridles to hamper the tongue
my mouth as soggy as an April flowerbed

the kernel in my chest arid but germinating;
Yumboe nannies cultivate suffrage

a modern rupture buds culture from their loamy palms
—our perduring shoots underwritten in bloom.

STAR / DATE

yesterday i was an astronaut cloistered in cosmic dust / today
my giraffe has wings & we wrangle a herd of white sheep
we entangle a horde of fascists in (or out of) white sheets

i'm a cacaoboy, *baby*
i'm a cacaoboy, *playa*

i'm down in the garden in my spacesuit tending my wife's
    tomato plants
constellational heirloom fruits dangle on the vine like
    a row of planets

i bite the fruit and blame the squirrels
my ray gun is burning hot and i'm missing home

the rocket door swings wide:
"the dumplins are done, baby; baby, come inside . . . come
    on inside, baby."

there is no greater gravity than love
"home" is where the orbit is & together we float in circles.

EBBONY

you bore witness reamed with receipts
pulled and swayed by every lunar phase
and stayed staring until dawn
fringed and dazed in reflective gleam
but *haughty moonlight* (it's said)
will only speculate the sun near eventide
her vainglory (as usual) waxing & rhapsodic—

> *hark!* you ants & tax accountants
> prosaic seamstresses & balmy daydreamers
> gather your fanny packs ladened with
> tape measures & telescopes
> applying fisheye to fantasy
> step forward & constellate your rhyme
> stalk & bray our Sweet Moon with
> the calipers of poetry's abating appraisal
> until your mucking sweet-talk takes orbit
> & lurches into soundtrack
> you eternal pallbearing putz you cosmos nut

yea she tugs at sea verbatim with vanity
plaintive for attentions cyclical in procession
but wake up dolt you're in a faze & on fire!
has she ever once pulled at your dulcet gaze
peeling back *your* sheets to share hot flashes

or a cold sweat? no. never has your ravenous moon
left a tithe upon your shores swearing to sear your name
in suffocating ode but every poet is a gibbous oaf

yes your steps *are* very small you fink
enjoyed to have scraped your knees against
her pockmarks & landscapes and daring
to halloo your lyrics as entitled leap
for all kind men you wretch you laughingstock
you corpulent linchpin for ebbonic lycanthropy
come and wane now within demulcent dark side
home free anywhere your fool head rises.

HOW TO REPAIR A GOOD BOOK'S BINDING

the soft brown leather
like my little bible / her
knees caressed open

to fondle the spine
the thumb strumming through pages
kissing the loose leaf.

UMBERJACK

i cannot for anger
or for my thirst for non-anger
but i can (and

continually have)
cut out the entire furnace of my throat—
    my aubergine tongue / stunned

& far-flung towards a sea i will never swim
nor sail: my distended voice
a literary paroxysm—

    sea-foams thrash in the mouth thrushed in sorrow
    poems cast nets at the solar & my fasting shadow
    distills pedagogical sun into souse / overly erudite

my aubergine tongue
seeded in the bleak
until it spates the dawn

and come morning i amble
in overgrown byways of thought
sequestered safely from declensions in hope

gilded fleurs-de-lis in halo / strings of daisies
in my denim cuffs *& bat wings!?* goddammit
from nape's allaying kitchen i've sprouted the blackest of wings!

i surge forward carnal & clergy to write what is wrought
off-centered with ribcage the credenza for moon
dreams capsized in honey / dreams capstoned by ancient umbra

and from such an undulating brine i rime
singed with songs of surgency & surrection / every vow
oppressively eclipsed with insatiable brightness

my anger & my calm—
2 dope buoys on a cataract
termagant. halcyonic.

i dare you name one other
with abbeys cobbled from crucible
or chapels built from jeopardy

GRAVEYARD VENTRILOQUISM

my soul wades an astral swamp to concuss
what's green like God smears their oily thumbprint
on Gaia's jade canvas, my black statue
of thought dark as a jackal's ass and as
grainy as Death's toothsome grin: autumn caught
in Thoth's haggard grip until winter. like
a nocturnal moss I coil tow'rds chaos
spewing embers & ash until the day
I lay flat in jarred motif—the molten
afterthought in a closed casket wildly
bellicose briefly volcanic. in the
media of soul my simmering smile
reflects a shimmer and tho you might hear
my ardent laughter in brusque eruption
you'll never know the locus of my mind
how dusk night-edits the miscellany
of my heart yowling for Arcadia.

MENDING THE NETS

in a house i'll never own i've built a boat
within the boat a gleaming rocket
within the rocket a temple

stone within steel within wood within brick
within within / a sfumato of breath / *within within* / *always within*

seven hulls deep i kneel & pray to be made the sky
each prayer an ocean of glass

within this poem i've built a mill
from the soils i've built an obstreperous sea . . .

with which fabrics shall i make tomorrow?
of what ontologies shall i mend my nets?

A NIGHT IN TUNISIA (ALTERNATE SOLO)

your body is my
bazaar—swap-meet's black t'rific
an allaying love.

ELEGBA ON THE PLAYGROUND ERECTOR SET

I know
I am / but
what are
you?

a black breath caressing darkness
in a closed heart.

I know
I am / but
what are
you?

love: seeking life in the fallen petals
of a woman's palm.

I know
I am / but
what are
you?

a man. just a man; in his natural state and
brown as fuck / like the backbone of a rainbow

tho I stand
on a mound of deep
sorrows I sing

what am I?

my hipbones
a doubled wreath
of Saint George's sword

what am I?

a whetstone
a father's hum
a bowstring tautly strung

what I am

a savanna son
arching through open sky's
argent door

THE OCCUPYING PARABLE OF THE SILVER-SPOON PURGATORY

to roll in the ashes
of your brother and
the skull of your mother
(once bleached of imperfection)
—*a cupholder for capitalism:*

white gloved & pinkies out
Death's Head with its appallingly
bright teeth pins you to Freedom
it challenges you to act indignant
yet still you dare be discomfit
by your captors' loud laughter
your prayers ingratiated
to the self-immolation of tears—

the ley bent by fault line into a sleeper cell.

meanwhile:

our shadows incensed
on the outskirts of town
flicker against the night.

ROSETTA POEM

your children don't see you when you
lack imagination (and neither does the world)

all they see are the clothes on your back—made
elsewhere by hands you've never held or known

othered myths stitched across your shadow
borrowed folklore as comforter for your fading imprints

under lampposts druids in fairytale catcall your poems—
no avowing eye contact *nor even* the simple head nod

in black disclosure just your immaterial soul discretely
escorted to an enervated baptism down by the river.

VANISH IN OUR SLEEP

for Pillow

-1-

stargazers when the stanzas break . . .
black skins that pierce night like an Eye of God,
our breaths heavy with lullabies wet as pot-liquor
hang thick in our throats 'til combustion—
a molten spell

and in the belly of my head I hunger you
and see the sorghum (if not the glory)
in your Genesis. all the heavens in affirmation . . .

. . . an *aflammation?*
how (already) are we not jambalaya & allegory?
there is no retardant in the air we can't resist

—an Igbo charm airborne between us—

Kichawi in love's birthright & it is beautiful
until there's only spit against skin in a night
of ablution our tongues to do the lifting
abscising body into song my palms entangled
at your nape in its thickets 'til I'm begging
for your pokeweeds & their imperfections
and lay my scales down before you
your bowl spilling coffees on my sauce plate
where I'm tithing at your feet
muscle stretching into muscle into muse . . .

I only want us un-famished

it's that simple.

to see us *Golden & Carnal*
and in this vein *We Are Cosmic.*

-2-

solemn in this solstice / somber for your solace
the Sun in our Hearts and me begging you & all
your Creators to raise their tines & eat of me
our candescent mercies transmogrifying
in this gullet of night / glancing from
your singing lap in call to worship / my clarion
throat in full flower, shouting from every garden
knee-deep at the base of towers that keep you:

Assata! Mercurial Assata!
Let Down Your Nappy Hair!

[titty to tongue; all of me wherever you want
whenever you need / all of us / whatever this is,
whoever we are / day or night / ears to loins]

-3-

let us prick our hands
with spindled oath & merge
interwoven with morn
towards tumbled dream.

THE LIGHTHOUSE AT THE BOTTOM OF THE OCEAN

how long have we stood this close to extinction
our two horizons out of sync

our kisses fossilized as time
calcifies in our hearts?

dust flares on the surfaces we share
like a meteor skims the moon

our debris winking in the sunlight
tossing parmesan throughout the darkness

Garçon! Saturn shouted, his mouth full of pate,
his progenital pâté *(Gaea herself held phobias for just such occasion)*

what is this erasure of the terrestrial haven
in which we bask? / I'm politely asking

how does a planet this lush quake apart
while Lords and their Prophets bask quietly in the pale?

LITERARY DADAISM INFOMERCIAL

the water hose runs all day
its dulcet fluids biting. unabated.
and every surface saturated until heavy as death
resulting in obeyance & pleasure
and addiction to hunger.

* *but wait!* **there's more!** *

new love is a bucket of light
old love is a bucket of sand
dedication is but a bucket of buckets

* *not one, not two...* *you get four!* *

I planted both ears and grew a groundswell,
a sinkhole . . . my pronoun is a pinecone. call me
a unicorn, call me a taxi cab . . . tongue is a hermit crab.

Captain Ahab is my profile pic / no, no.
my gender is Jean-Luc Pequod—a pod of wails . . .
(blandlocked: my gender a boulder, my caul a rod)

landlocked
like a landmine
I'm a landline . . .

** yours for 3 easy payments of ~~$79.95~~ $49.95! **

don’t you yet see?

I plant both eyes to grow a beholder.

anywhere I seed my hands a preface flowers.

FIRST INTERMISSION

laying in the dark
and it is not death
nor even an accoutrement of death
laying without the accoutrements of light
within grief—is this a body?
or is this (right now)

even   *a poem?*

my wish is for grieflessness
to be a body of dark laying down
upon me with all the tragic audacities
of a building bombed:

the sky failed
our sighs fallen

our mouths lip-synched to ruin in prayer.

ERRFBOUND

the cold air's veracious so i tighten up my collar
balled fists are as charcoal bricks in the pockets
of a bomber jacket where *The Modern Black Poem*
comes wrapped in mental foil like a whiting sandwich
from the fish fry the rising sun a hot sauce packet
waiting to be opened *but alas* my favorite barber
no longer takes walk-ins—*ain't that a bitch!*
a bemoaning mane of many flames my scraggly beard
an avalanche in white stuck in suspended animation

and because i never learned to ghazal enough i curse
& fisticuff as relaxation in the depths of daydream
ah. if mouth only knew to guzzle some incredible
epistle casting in parable the mechanics of black
phrasing perhaps then i could amplify this dirt-drawn
imploding self-celadon i drone on and on about:

i'm the poet i've come to split the pole
to aerate moldy history with cold hysteria
until our shared verdigres are pervasively
enunciated so (as i navigate this levee) *come*
partake of this gravel-mouthed hearth
of my tomatoes & my purslanes until all
are sated or else in seminal disgust our
distended bellies turn in great aversion
my very sides hurting at the sight of you.

i till until at last at the bottom of throat: a quarto
its arid black rasp thickens & sprouts jejune i keel
into this garden my pylon of lungs distilled
by whinnied laugh and i dissolve into the dusk
where *(on paper)* every verse is cheval-de-frise
ready for the fight—the earth moon and every
disparate star above aligned dragging and clanking
from my heels like tin cans on a celestial wire

TO HAINT BY NUMBERS

the kettle boils but when's the last time a wicked witch
wrote their liner notes with a coffin nail? each hex

over-contextualized and bored certified by a lettered provost.
the authors who write a nonlinear nightfall have tared to zero

and now we all pledge Kappa Alpha Coven having sold
every cauldron to a coffee roaster and now it's *eye of newt*

& toe of frog in a secondhand air fryer. how do you even cast
the proper spell when your entire house lacks cast iron?

never curse an ex-love using a nonstick skillet unable to afford
the high cost of favoritism *The Old Head Black Poet* sits on

the roadside waiting to be discovered by algorithms my apologies,
cherished *Circe,* I plea forgiveness, precious *Hecate* but this hex

smells a wee spoiled and if the reexamined breath proves rancid
is reimbursement too much to ask if I show my bills of sale?

AE'QUAN'S FABLE

tortoise has my tongue

(sloe & heady whens the race)

your hare's in my face

THE DEVIL'S DULCIMER

or Concatenation Noir

in my dream, the moon
was three days waning
three quarters pale and orange dripping
me towards orbit. i was a stone-cold sickle
swinging like a wild wild
west-african gunslinger,
my hammer gilding gold into southern art.
i jumped the tracks between imacs and boxcars

pale and orange, i stepped out the flames,
burnt but otherwise unscathed; hellfire knelt
and called me king of the juju jesuits.
my kofi cocked to the side, i rocked
a kenté-colored jumpsuit.

jimi hendrix,
eddie hazel,
& junior kimbrough:
my 3 magi / a witchdoctor mosaic.
they bade i make a banjo
digging for misplaced tongues &
buying back black souls when all
other bluesmen was just a business
begging & bartering from eshu elegbara's
pristine ledgers for borrowed time.

i was born with a mouth made to wax and wane;
dark words more than mud my new-age sankofa
pulled by moon. the earth my modem
and i spat out its dirty dissonance
the divarication of darkest africa
where rem and brainstem combine.

    and then it all came rushing back,
    a conscientiousness regained.

the hypnotist's dulcimer chimed 7 times.
"so what exactly do you remember?"

rubbing the sleet from my eyes i said,

well, my wife had gathered dung for the fire,
our children rustled goats then came with water.
i was over by the cattle enjoying the breeze.

i believe i was standing; atop a wooden stool i stood.

orunmila gave a warning:
desiccation came running; famine entered
me like a fable & stayed for centuries.
on the front of my t-shirt: "proust-face killah"
i was a barista. i sold used books.

then you were standing there, doc,
dragging with you a darkness.

shadows stirred the dust

there was outburst and communal crying.
smoke and pyre and the smell of urine,
then suddenly, angle swallowed sphere.

my mouth as if from rain filled
with foreign symbols; the sea sang our song
but pretended not to know me.

and then you, doc, you
leered above. deck high.
i lay far below. in chains snaking into a void.

doc dropped his pen reaching for his phone.
he squinched and squozed. tapped & pinched
told me to say cheese as i froze . . .
"in remembrance," he smirked.
from some app he quoted oaths—wrinkled words
for some unsavory curse or incoming calamity.
abruptly, his mustache grew & began to curl,
his bifurcated tongue wagging,
downloaded monologues
for my ascent or my demise?

chair metal sparked skidding against
the floor's wood grain: my fists bracing,
fingers shrinking into palms

"we knew this day would come," doc said,
"the mighty sun slivering through the cracks,
memory shivering. pushing and shoving
towards center. reversing exodus
every forgotten odu reopened.

well, ain't nothing left now but the crying.
out the frying pan / the shit hitting the fan and all;
    master plans and whatnot.
auf wiedersehen, motherfucker.
all your base are belong to us."

the air between us cracks,
every shadow a whirling dervish / but sankofa
revolved the door & orunmila stepped out
into the light—my laughing liberator;
his song a shield, his poems protecting
he touched me on my forehead, my faud in flames:

"FOR YOU I POINTED TOWARDS DESTINY
BUT ALL YOU SAW WERE TWINKLING STARS, NOT
YOURSELF. IT'S NOT YOUR FAULT; WE FORGIVE."

when canonizing zeus,
africa's cavalries get overlooked.
but every song is self-lionizing.
the self-aggrandizing of ghosts
so when backed into cataclysm
countercultures will prevail
& very few will see it coming:

folktales intact (check).
spiritual gps rerouting (check).
my 'nations sack is full and
not only am i face-to-face
with tomorrow, i'm now
matter-of-fact
with my entire past.

BLACK NATURE: POEM

once the conversation is fertile
i plant my teeth—the small seeds
for growing skull; the vegetal moon
offered not its incessant rind,
but even tho i'm still bereaved & ill behaved,
please, in full, forgive, i beg:
for never once did i sup on fennel.

*

after all, i am poet: i calcify & i kernel.
my persona of grit & grain an inhospitable grift

black, my kneads;
unknelt, still black   / & yet:

the leaves of autumn stacked, in deck,
withheld their promise; undealt. unkind.

how solemn, my golem of words, might now
appear, but don't you see? my rind of occipitals in soil

already in bloom? so let's prepare our belletristic
garden, *Kind Lich,* its inconsolable graft:

the autumn sun ascending
behind my orbital brow.

for reprise? as reprisal? either way, my ethereal love
a trowel & the hilt of its blade a perennial anger.

BEDSIDE SLOP JAR

you've come this far,
my dear, majestic reader,
my sweet, indiscrete miscreant,
so why abandon us now?

glory awaits;   the valor—*all yours.*

you can cringe beneath the clarion,
crinkled within the twilight—or other
claw your spurs into my soft black rump
pulling up the rear on steadied steed
clamanting *CHARGE!* as time-spent calvary
or gallant martyr for your invidious bookclub
                                                  or whatever

so get off your cushy ass
decant more wine, savor
the discordance (ambrosia or slop)
and turn the page to continue the glory.

CELESTIAL ROMANCE THEORY

•

they say that the tears of Black Women carry
too much heat, but we neglect in full vocation her stilly sigh—
refuse to recognize its weightless light borne from womb
but if it anguishes? that's well assigned:
                    reams & scrolls
                    scientific journals
                    the hard, poetic tome
where we misalign & deny her romanticisms for woe
confuse her effusive pause as unwanted wander
ignoring any Black Woman's dissertation
on chamomile tea & ostrich fans infused with lavender
instead, seeing how, after all, she is "extremely strong"
so we rally and crown her in tired tragedy—here, sis,
have hope; eat, sis, this hearty soup; take, sista,
this heavy, brotherly shrug and brace yourself
because God never gives you more than you can handle
—we prophesy & communion for Black Calamity;
hardly stoop to stop for soft, never scoop to swaddle
the Black Tear in supplication—our reserved totalitarianism
for abject beauty (just not the Black Distraction:
a cultural aesthetic robbed of supernal abstraction)

your suffering smells too floral, sis;
sister, you getting enough fiber in your diet?

this is why Isabella Baumfree became the first American sibyl.

• •

tears roil from our eyes like smoke
rolling from under door but what are we to do?
if it's black it must be ominous—
    a putrescent wine in hoary basin
or insignificant—
    the putrescent wine of antagonists in orbit
we do not commune a reverence to Black Skin

• • •

but i look at you & what i am learning to say:

i see.

the sightliness. how serene. the downy love
in all you do; your radiance dreamy & delicate . . .
the overlooked allure of black sublimity
the lavender in our lamentations

• • • •

the ink wells up within you & i see it
offer the papyrus of palm for note-taking, in witness—

your spirit a captivating smudge
suspending at my shoulder:

it engulfs me, this miry constellation
these deep wet stars i see bobbing along your cheeks

but i'll never reduce what pangs you to pedestal;
your epos is eternal . . .

Sweet Adulant, please, come to me . . .

no, no, you've been eternal now for 10,000 years;
allow me, my dear, this coming to you in pleasure

—the sinuous river gushing towards the gulf.

BAS-RELIEF 3

your smile
a soft simile
a tender siphon.

. . .

GIVE THE DRUMMER SERMON

after Bearden's collage, Of the Blues: Kansas City 4/4 *(1974)*

I teleport ancestrally; time travel celestially
through black skin / my tongue a Tardis or
shapeshifting djembe my black bones a scurvy
or a dervish; a dust storm aswirl
—if you will

so drop & give the drummer some or better yet,
stop & listen as the drummer gives *sermon*
to his audience braised on hardship; a bruised brew.
but if not a Tardis then a railcar, our songs
self-infused across the rings of Saturn; so surrender,
Sweet Maestro / our *Suite Muezzin*
—if you will

to the snare of a 4/4 science / a transmogrifying
spell using the blues to break time: Chronos
in the cubism of the afrosurrealist; and yes, for
the percussionist, anti-stillism was always a tangible
commerce while many corpse-drone-machines done
drummed Soul's *Internal Ephemerides* in sidereal time;
witnesses *(and Faust Prophets)* to "the unseeable"
but some black holes done observed the charred up
poet up close for ages; a solar aureola blues
—if you will

some entire galaxy's corona rolled up in a reefer
dangling from the lips of the azure as it reassembles
welkin Gods center-stage / turning ashes of dysphoria
into rhythms of open flame; a nascency of Ayan Agalu
in American doo-wop / a billet-doux quartet
          —*if you will*

or   *if you will*—
the Genesaic percussion from
Babalú-Ayé's planetary nebula;
you know, just creation's penumbral
collage grabbing at your collar.

ALTAR-ATIONS

for Pillow

in the deepdark
your gravel drawl is
all the shawl I need.

a midnight borealis your blackness is
as America boils your bounty from the bone
trying to clone you / to un-cling us
from melody, wanting to cleave you
cleanly from the oncoming horizon.

but only God could trap the daylight colors
that comprise you, cascading into the dark
kaleidoscope your gentle heart harbors.

Olodumare's hands are a cornucopia
to encircle you / a living licorice his hands,
molding you into the warm solstice
folding upon me as we sleep. a moist
clabbered sorcery your complete softness is.

ensconced in your sweet darkness
I am made the most divine / and
what a tithe you are against my tongue:

oh, what a religious thing
our rugged beauty—
a Genesis between lips.

FAYRE GABBRO, TRUBL HELIX, & THE JUMP ROPE OF DEATH

we can't see it from earth (you'll need light years / centuries away) but our sun is one of 19 stars in the Double-Dutch Constellation; our Sol is the heel of Olodumare caught in jumped-rope ascension / mid-air. the twin handlers, Fayre Gabbro and Trubl Helix, sister-warriors always one-upping.

Gabbro's guessing games often end with death and Trubl's plaits, long and stiff as a ray of light extend from her scalp to poke, two planets away, the ears and eyes of any Orisha in passing.

the Twins were always underfoot, "worsem" said cousins and uncles. but when their mountain village was overrun with accosting hordes from the lowlands, the Twins' superior skills at Double-Dutch, thence, saved the day.

they danced as they jumped, quaked earth as feet thumped the ground; their ropes, in steady swishing, destroyed all opposers. from a distance, those with spyglasses called it "creation" . . . but those in the know simply called it "their usual commotion."

as the story goes, Trubl Helix now races dirt bikes and runs a daycare; Fayre Gabbro is a doula with her wicked-witch-in-training certificate, and is a "subversive yoga instructor" (whatever that is) at her local Y.

they together form a punk band: *Chakra Khan:* tambourines and futuristic flute samples with oblations of drum & bass / folk dirges and funk ditties piercing ripples / twin dervishes trafficking in dark matter and boson tea particles, emceeing all commencement ceremonies for the dark-hued protagonists at the debutantes' ball.

BAS-RELIEF 4

i'm concussed
beyond all composure
through alighted kiss
and the tectonic shift
of your slowly drifting palm.

. . .

BRING PIGS TO THE WEDDING

instructions for our indigenous matrimony

bring kava root & several pigs or you won't get in, security will beat you back with an ox tail switch (if not shank you—*outright*—with a bamboo shaft)—it's our rural way / no exceptions. bring shea & aged bourbon or short-storied books & Advil gel-caps for the bride *(we've gotten gray)*. in your swag bag: rhubarb & rutabaga. & a bartender serves coconut shakes out by the garage / out by the garage, we'll prance & dance hard til the banana tree drops & the nefarious Meadowthorpe Neighborhood Association comes at us with their infernal codebook extended & damning yellow banners / bask, mannered guests, in this Black Beauty—*our prized possession,* this celebration of *ceremony*—as when rituals came perforation-free, before outsider-smudge called our reverential rites *vestigial* // if the grass is wet then daddy's Hoveround will lose traction, so keep an eye on the sacrificial cow slipping her knot or else we'll all dine on Indi's chicken wings, potato wedges, & sour greens instead of tender beef baked underground on hot stones (also keep watch on Joi & Kevin—*we hear you, we support you* but *this* banquet wedding is no place for animal activism) / traditions come new in diaspora yet a few feel vintage by default — the goal: for free-range to feel homegrown, for the modern invention of *3-piece & a biscuit* to transcend *Holy in Heritage* // daddy too will slaughter a sow as dowry for his daughter-in-law's people but since the bride no longer eats pork (unless it's peppered) the groom's mama will have turkey bacon on standby in the microwave & what cookout is complete without chickpea burgers hot off the grill? (Joi & Kevin—*these aren't just for you*) there'll be gazelle games for the fleet of foot & ghazal poems for the quickest of wit: our lottery system for picking partners in whist or spades / 17 Orishas will be the judges & competition will be fierce, so maintain your altars early & often // the procession starts at 10 a.m. / bare are the breasts of the bridesmaids but that's nary an issue: *no snark, no shame* / with doilies as dashiki fringe / this tissue-covered juju—for ours is both an indigenous & an Instagrammed aesthete // the bride *(that's little Crissy. Crystal. or Crys)* rides forth in a rockaway, adorned in the amber gauze of sunshine's vibrant gaze; then the grown men from her mother's side will carry Crissy from her carriage, yay high in a gilted litter, held aloft like some new-era Nefertiti—just as aunties open pots & gourds in choir, placating the Gods with cooking songs that stimulate the soul: cast-iron communions that pay tribute to our Egun because nothing says "sermon" like an old iron skillet / a good foo-foo knows the pestle's favorite hymnal—the *krik? krak!* of mortar & memory / every ritual full of sweet-potato pie, milk-cake, & double-barreled rye. it's surreal, but even in Kentucky we have camels—a remnant, it's said, of the Ohio River Slave Trade *(only Olodumare knows if that shit is true)* and over near Weisenberger's Mill, seven llamas give their life to Auset & Shango while the groom *(that's me, little Ronnie: Hello, I'm Ronald; you can call me Dirt)* and all his men ride in from the east on a herd of buffalo borrowed from former neighbors in Woodford County, the kind of place where country bibles are berthed from a Gayl Jones diary // it's sad, but many a modern woman rebuke the old eras & refuse the making of hay-skirts from the great lawn, so blue denim replaces bluegrass *(shit, some traditions just have to change)*; Elegbara sweeps in from the shadows, Aunt Mildred comes up from Franklin, Aunt Elizabeth comes in from La Grange; fried cabbage and country quilts are spread from kitchen to curb while the Woodford County Women's Group reenact just how a young Harriet Tubman used those same quilt designs leading sun-people out of sunlessness // as 6 p.m. approaches, the 24-hour ceremony begins to shorten: the barefoot groom looms nearer his intended-to-be sharing African vows under a Victorian porch; they'll repeat traditional verses before a state-licensed babalawo, their two voices clinging off-key, ringing as one, warding away any offended witch portending drought because summer-warm sunshowers are better night magic for a luminous matrimony / and the August rain falling gently atop nappy heads is a much better custom than throwing uncooked beans & rice squarely into the eyes.

I Do. You Do. We All Do.

a broom is jumped—then bride & groom bend their bodies into rainbow. lend each other daylight & offspring / granddaughter-tomboys grow into flower-girls who feign obedience; grandsons in mock defiance throw gardenias against the ground (still wishing instead for firecrackers and footballs) / the babies will chase fireflies after sunset then recess inside for counting games on sesame-street.org, eating the ice cream churned vigorously & blessed by the brow sweat of Black women: the whole choir from New Creation African Lutheran Church ("that building with Black Jesus painted 30 feet on the side?", "yes, but that's really Black Moses; it confuses people." // after sunset we all recess // full of neon the newlyweds recede into a Kalakuta ritual—a miscegenation of Fela Kuti, Roberta Flack, & Marvin Gaye, our blue lights dimming in the basement until there is a mash-up of moaning: redemptive love songs mixed with levee camp melodies / how beautiful their hues / *what a miraculous bounty her hand within his* // there's no "pray tell" only their dark, abiding privy. and then, aroun' midnight: outside, *duskdark,* the families dance, trancing hard until dawn approaches & the baobab tree breaks freeing the spirits trapped within to come sing extemporaneously / keeping our connubial tales not-so-close to the vest; a nest of parables in bloom & blossoming hearts / yes, new rhythms wax & wane under a watchful eye / Anansi descends in wisdom from the moon, offers honeycomb & laughter, offers of Aché from our ancestors—*yes, yes*—the blessings are indeed abundant / oh how beautiful our blessings—but absolutely nothing is as resoundingly replete as *this* is: this this is: *our forever-living love.*

CANON FODDER

chapter 1

protected by parables
I sic my books on you
flip *Double Trio* like a brick
Good Woman in the small of my back like a glock
I Am a Cowboy in the Boat of Ra is my gang sign

Fred Moten paces rooftop
training poem flocks
like homing pigeons;
Rammellzee is in the bake shop
mixes roots into writ

chapter 2

an older cousin was El Rukn (retired)
bragged about they carried rocket launchers
set ready for *any* The Revolution
(post-hippie, pro-black, pre-sellout The Warriors)
—I was related to Osiris in real life . . .

> *a gang of black poets is called pointless,*
> *a mixed metaphor, an orisha's epiphany.*

chapter 3

the IRS kicked in my bookstore's front door
called my writings a sophist contraband
handcuffed my laptop and our coffee cups

feds director read my works in progress
calling each dramatic meme a manifesto
the overhead light hithered to and fro / vertigo triggered
by the shadows in swirl, a cavalcade of sweat on my face . . .

they read me my rites & asked if i was *with attitude*
"your attempt to Ghazal is down the hall spillin' its guts,
but tell us what you know & we'll cut you a deal"

they slammed a golden shovel down on the table / but

MOTHERFUCKER, I SAID I AINT NO GLITCH!
I never seen such logodaedaly before in my life, officer.

AFTER 3 LONG YEARS AN ANTAGONIST TIPS HER BARISTA

the blacks of my eyes wholly eclipse my soul
and in the dawning of this love the shadows
in my heart are forced torrentially ajar.

our communion in fine fettle, the kilter corrected
we together wallow in the exoneration; the leaf turned
anew, a thread of heather where once was blight.

MENTAL TALE-APATHY

some come to poetry for its
perpetual motion for its buxom beauty
for the truvia of its mind-control searching
for the hint or the hindrances of freedom
for the certainty of unbreakable insight

some for mutually assured self-destruction
for love's quantum trivia / a thesaurus of old gods
burned at the stake with the bones of grief
as its kindling for who but the spiritually ill
come with sorrows reeking to the poetry reading
searching for solace in the written grift
of solidarity & kindness?   *some.*

but in truth: *there's no begging in poetry—*

angels & devils unravel the planet as your favorite
slave spits in your tea   *or*   you swallow
your tongue & abandon the antidote

either way:

whether you bleed out beneath a raptured moon
or with the saliva of abolition on your avocado toast
you're gonna eat this fucking poem   and
you're gonna learn to fucking like it.

AWKWARD HUSBANDRY

this fairy tale is in Mingus-mode praising
its own sinful symphony, pleading its case
for sainted heresies, bleeding ruined words
into the void / this space-rover crashing
into the dark side of the moon. just look
how my paints plead their darker colors first:
contaminating with ejecta later the lighter layers . . .
its botched spells splatching experimental colors
—I was trained this way to write, informed by
out-of-body haints; not by the *nudge / wink / wink*
of some epistemic hierarchy but by the conch call
from a much higher exegesis. you see, bootblack
was the nightgown for my psychotic break;
a signifying monkey   *(my orisha's crown is)*
suggesting I set language aflame in every
orphanage for the 3rd-eye blind / my words
ache using crayon to draw dot matrix
within the open margins inside the pages
of *Jet* and *Ebony* magazines, penning poems
in paper's white creases with the gristle
from SAMO'S same ol' pinky bone because
there is no priggish graffiti without first
robbing graves. the *proper gander* of impolite
blackness. my graphite cells cloning self,
the wolf who cried "BOY!" because lycanthropy
is all in the language, some soft ~~silver bullet~~

silvery bullshit but only after bitten. and then
off cue: every slogan sheds a sheepskin:
howl movements to woo your mother, her hutch
breached, her hymns clutching at drawls and
pearls / what a torch song this hairy man's tongue;
these self-afflicted words give you the moon
and its infection—a full-time tune, but tender,
an over-pouring of vice and individual verdict;
the judge's vinyl decree: *—DEATH!—*
by heavy breathing; this triangular-trade-in-reverse
copping a feel on the breast of age-old adages;
the born-again love song recalibrating itself
on the playing field.   *Figaro, Figaro . . .*
but niggaro, what exactly are you saying?

BAS-RELIEF 5

your tears
into my open palms
until they clot:

that is more than i can hope;
you rooting within,
my lungs a lyceum for us.

. . .

POEM TO SLAY CHICKENS TO

yes. I am a shanty; my forgotten faith has made a lean-to
of language; black culture from a centuries-old deluge,
a misdiagnosed black holocaust turns on its notifications
/ a blackness that said-saviors refuse to document:

> "if, indeed, you've sustained such a hurt,
> as you say, so-called, then prove it: where
> are the papers for the pains you claim?"

our makeshift roofs of outrage are nothing if not reliable;
but who is our landlord? who is it we call for maintenance?
it always comes back to my tin-can tongue
shingled in dark-skinned wisdom / singing
for soup, of bars of soap, and a longing for soapstone:

sacramental miracles

verse is safe space for solemn affairs; *voice has to eat*
and loves to cook. but, like everyone else (in our youth),
I too longed for many mansions and a gold-plated love.
but now, under-noon, beneath an ever-present sun
I thank Olorun for I know, now, exactly where I belong:
here.

it's always been here.

asphalt will succumb & mud ascend beneath
a slogging earth; its playful mood *a joyful mood.*
I won't sneak smoke into the conversation / clouding
your complaints of my comfort / if our asserted pains
will not be seen canonical then I will sleep at least,
in a clean bed, my yellowing teeth sinking into the societal
strain—for the hemoglobins have spoken and I must obey.
so I no longer ask you to look back / although it was indeed
bad form of you to invite us over only to deny us
the right to dine and now all the verdant wine between us
is spoiled and I'm left no choice but to reject such
a home-welcoming gift . . . this house is mine—
        get the fuck (please) *off my lawn.*
how else, neighbor, did you expect this last
century shared together drawing to a close?

GREEN-APPLE JOLLY RANCHER STICK BLUES

blkluv is gravitas & gritty and skins stuck
by mortars of sweat & spirit & *shonuffgood . . .*
you see, here in the creases, this is god

fingers pick & pry & poke the "I" out of love . . .
big lips branded by hipbone & blk thighs throb a poem.
is this god?. . .   oshit, this is *better* than god.

& we are not alone / you see, we have us / laying
back in the belly of darkness, a prophet &
a priestess / blk beauty & a bullshitter . . .

blk thighs do not open unto poem
no, they open unto prayer . . .
(& this is how we beget a legacy)

a juju & jolly ranchers knowledge / I am tenderly
reckless with a mysticism for candy necklaces . . .
there is tootsie roll to this romance & we are 6 again

& giddy . . . then 16. & yearning.   26   & 56.   106.
if this is better than god   then this *is* love
& in this absence of light, I

am again ready for our games:
"five, six . . . *pick up sticks*
seven, eight . . . *don't be late."*

HAULING ASP (A SHEA BUTTER GOSPEL)

I am spirit-machine; 100 tons of soapstone
and cowrie shell and postmodern technology.
I am not the Shango app for an iPhone you want me to be.

7 generations removed, I am an Ashanti king wannabe
in dada sneakers shooting dice for ramens money between
the former mosque of troublesome black Muslims and
the used bookstore once a whites-only museum.

I was born in the year of the zombie
(according to a long-lost calendar of the Yoruba)

I am spirit-machine . . . machine-gun-runner-supreme;
there is Afro Sheen in my circuitry; my nano-sciences
glow and gleam; my motherboard teems with *songs*
to honor the dead by . . . the shoes of the fisherman's
wife is some jive ass slippers is my theme song and
a beatboxing Elegba is my ringtone—*such is my religion.*

I'm forever rhyming under rubble, squeezing blood from the blues.
I live on & on—the living loop sample of my ancestors.
but even Don Cornelius grew old and i have yet to have
The Sons and Daughters of Nat Turner's Bluesky page
follow back when I heart-thingie all of their posts:

I'm just a ghost of Malcolm X-mas past
hainting my inner self every Juneteenth Eve.

offer lotion for an elbow, I'll divine your fate within a poem.

CULLED BLACK POEM GOUACHE

in *urban ledging* the discarded
black poem ascends Ile-Ife:
shadowspace quilting

each word into a bucket of stars—
"constellational vèvès"
shouting *no one dare stop us.*

THIS ISN'T GOING TO END WELL......

-i-

is black and prosaic a sin?

-ii-

dreadlocks thread out
flared across the face of the fiddle

an indivisible god strums the strands
their atrous hands turning rhythm to wine.
the flames are fanned for our renaming:

this flame they call "you"

-iii-

this one they name "me."

a suture in the flesh / a fool for the taking.

-iv-

if the spirit is ruptured
then here I am: a goddamn poet / a sometimes painter
but if I cain't be your sinnersaint, then what good is love?
but love or hate—"to win or to lose" / I'm good either way

-v-

and if not a suture then I'm a scar . . .
just tar & feathers, philosophically so.
I'm blasé-logical when speaking of rapture—the czar tared to zero.

-vi-

introspective & inebriated
but not in the capacity of *iNigga*.
"fuck fate" is my audacious song:
nubian shanties by way of ancestors
caped in kenté & neon.

-vii-

I do not glitter / I glow *if there's a difference*

my tongue a truncated wand
to ward off invented darkness;
a negritude that cleaves away
the anatomically bleak from the fermenting
fatmeats of amelioratory blackness.

-viii-

called into account:
my coif coiled. my spirit soiled. my body broiled
in the breaths of gravitas & gris . . .
a human gumbo; my kettles
full of a kindness to kill for.

-ix-

I'm drawing lumps of coal with sticks of chalk . . .
this is my belief in a God we can not control.

-x-

banjos & djembes: that's all this is.

a houngan in overalls; high priest & hillbilly.
I'm a one-man jug band die-cast as universe.

outer space / outer shape.

that's all that I am.

screenname: *nap / kink / kohl.*

black and prosaic; cracked, but beautiful. a nyeusiphile.

mama says
I might be
damaged . . .

never has she said she didn't drop me.

BAS-RELIEF 6

let me condemn heaven
to hold you & tho i'm not one
to unusually risk eternal hell
i beg for no guarantee:

gift me whatever's frivolous
or most infinitesimal
that i may win you and not waste ruin,
left abandoned under lamplight
trading rhymes with the eternal.

let us softly render bodies
until all of us is less than marrow
then ply our mortal gels with
roaring lyric until we sleep,
prying fires from the flux.

. . .

SECOND INTERMISSION

i can't escape into
(or from) the earth.

i've tried.

but the nebulous spiraling portal of sorrow
that cherished gaslight within my chest
is always open / my languishing herald

"yes, that! write of grief, regrets (if not relief)
that the sorrowed might identify"

::

the boat sinks . . . they sing
astutely their indentions;
i mélange within.

THE APOCRYPHAL KENTUCKY ALEATORY BLUES

onetwo

wait. let me take & tell you:

I know I'm the pawn, I don't mean
to bring breakadawn to the story
hauled into account by some ancient agency
I'm not your "intellectual"—*there's been a mistake.*

I'm not the one you caul upon / this is not an allegory,
    I'm not   a-poet-you-like™.
I do not incite griots or riots
I'm a quiet vandal / asunnuva-sphinx;
I offer no indelible disco (not like that one one poet)
I speak an invisible ink,
a deciduous cipher / so understand me:
I am not the type of mothership
taking you to the stage—I swing low like Sweet Harriet
and if anyone told you I was their hat block of choice,
then obviously they have bad taste, *lissen here!*

if I lead you to a misunderstanding it's intentional.
I've always been "the pied pauper"—the backseat poet.

consider yourself took and tole!

wait. what? these old things?

this golden crown? I found it in the dump.
my marble throne? a yard sale.
this diamond scepter just fell from the sky
(some fallen angel threw it at me!)

HA!
ha, ha . . .

but see, wha-huh-happenedt wassss . . .

hey, look out that window!!

Chester Grundy is being
attacked by a grandiose gang!
Quickly—*let's all to his side!*

the ancestors do not abide slander to grand-elders!

onetwo, onetwo

many already speak in moods wet with indigo,
but I no longer offer voice to protest song . . . I don't belong
except to give tooth to power; that's a literary fine print.

so, no reaching into throat for bloated faith & its placebos.
no begging the unjust for solace or drum solos
no containeramilk, stickabutter, loafabread . . .
I will not commemorate solidarities
of near-convenience, placed on boozy display
like semi-shadows in bougie art museums:

        my honey supplanted with sulphur;
        I will not bojangle the beat
        with feet to ass in 3/5ths yoga.

no sir . . . no lip service; me no talk jive
attempting to incite jaundice in magistrates
        find some other lackey!
I will not expose opposable thumb to disposable dancing—
salving the feet of icons with Kool-Aid and calling it Jergens
assaulting sacrilegious moon with dollar-store homages
like make-believe federalists
for our own *Empire within an Empire*

                    —JARGONAUTS!

   but . . . if I was a poet? no, no . . .
   if I was anything other than a poet?!
   sweejeezus! *can you just imagine?*

            oh, fuckin' shit!
            fuckin' OMG!
            ZERO fkn MILLIGRAMS!

HERODIVERGENCY

1.
this endeavor of dreamstuff
of dust to dust: this diaspora a commodity

where black boys cannot believe in elves
or see themselves as superman

2.
where asphalt physically composes fantasy
the black wizard whispers "sankofa"

you mean, *like the coffee?*

3.
black arms unfold from wings
inflicted by a lack in affection
and are sharpened into tusks

from once face-first into the wind
to fist-first, not inflight, but infighting
jutted arms charge into serrated dream

wassup? wassup?—& away!

4.
who dared abuse the aura of black children?
praisesong for the african american mastodon
and his tarpit masculinity . . .

5.
it was our joy for two-square
that lifted us from the stone age
and ore—who smelt it dealt it

6,
fuck "a man of steel"
we need archeologists
burn this glacier down.

NKISI-EYED COUNTRY GIRL

the Ohio River grants her its skin / blackbright,
not dull like darkness / but in reflection of celebratory gods:
creation sculpted from the clay banks of midnight waters
until plain words are ceremonial:

a nkisi in the cornbread

her fro blooms with its own atmosphere
like a nimbus bulb / a comb of baobab tucked
in tangent atop her quintessential coils / a keepsake
hidden in high hip pocket of God

her nimble beauty
(inspiration for armed revolt when times, like now, are ripe)—
a worth rife with soft tongues

*

one would have to be an abacus or anemometer
measuring the jet stream between Côte d'Ivoire
and the backroads of Kentucky / would have to be
equal parts tobacco plant and elephant tusk;
a contemporary talisman

squint your eye and she is
Queen Tiye riding a Caterpillar;
a sharecropper of black resistance;
her womb a catacomb of languages lost,
be sweet and she may allow you to excavate.

*

there is Mary Magdalene, Marie Laveau,
& Mary McLeod Bethune within her / a pipeline
of Black Heritage distilling in her handbag:
acacia, poke root, deertongue / *double double toil and*
trouble fire burn and cauldron bubble / not Celtic-like
but how a country woman brews the blues. her tune hung
between Benin & Bowling Green / Liberia & Lynyrd Skynyrd
Harriet Tubman & Hatshepsut / hips that contour
history pushing spirited hymn from soulful hymen.

*

women like her are not strangled with preoccupation
straggling premonitions against "the struggle"

so if you hold its tail she'll milk the cow

*

sup from the rinds of a country girl
and you will not shoe-polish yourself / allow her love
to subjugate (if only once) and it's then
your fugues are lifted

unshackled you shall soar
and you will like it / *iswairfogawd.*

MONSTROUS ENLIGHTENMENT

my nonconformity
is entirely malleable
and i am wholly owned
by the ancestral hands
that forge me . . .

until i too is a god
and fully inalienable
to the self-exemplary;
no sham / no ire.

the black voice
is a technology of totems
a masonry of tongues
a symphony of umbras

uncalibrated parables &
phrases devoid of fear or fathom

our poems, swollen with
monstrous enlightenment
spew the nebulous
ndebelous in origin

in the hands of my egun
i become many gods
—divine + conquer.
no shame / no irony.

INTERIORITY INTERVENTION SUPPORT GROUP

should i write poems for you to know me
for you to know where i'm from?

"here is my spleen / over here i fingered
my first love" with a steeplechase of metaphors
running for the roses (the tequila & the rosé)

but i'm not here for new life or newfound
friends just to simply die here in the whirl
avoiding the blur; just for excavationists in
the future / digging into the sheetrock of me
looking into the sun, their parched lips
parting crevices across masks of clay,
a shield of hand / its shadow, to say

"oh shit.

more sheetrock!"

MYTHEMATICS

the same tongue that sings out to god and the egun
rings now with warning, a fever in the forehead of our voice:

> "heed my advice our neighbors are not themselves
> they come with nets & iron and other utensils
> to capture dignity but this pestilence is not their blame
> plague is brought to us from them *beyonderspirits*
> from those birthed on the wrong side of sunset
> the handiwork of a wretched pandemic
>
> our neighbors send us to uncertainty
> but feed your crowns for them—it was either
> *take this pound of salt & stalk of ginger for the flesh of others*
> or face picking cotton and stripping cane with their own
> feet in shackles their humanity tethered to bad brains
> like goats under the knife // our venerable myths slaughtered
> for its meat to the gods of white math our reverences
> perforated and called pagan it's sad but had contagion
> breached us first here in our homes then we'd be the ones
> betraying cousins in protection of our women and young
>
> grab your children your stash of yams, and run
> return too soon and you won't recognize the homecoming
> stay away until your steel is strong hold daylight in the small
> supple bowl of your back and when this new distress

comes again you'll return unbowed without bend
become the break of dawn and show this death the door

we don't need your horizon we already have our own

sankofa comes with the sun but it's azubuike that shines
for us   *so run* / runaway *now*   or fight & with our feasible
fists we escort assailants to their last fall of night unwilling to
let them rewrite our defiance as docile for there is no negotiating
with our destiny no negation of our eternal objections our free
spirits turned domesticated flame in their hearths the basin
of our skulls used as saucepans where they eat—

all people feed their ancestors at altar but for us to remain
sovereign then beneath these stars we starve their gods."

THE SHOES OF THE FISHERMAN'S WIFE

-insole-

the fish on my head tells its own story
it's umbilical tongue tethered to my heart.
its tale in my chest gasping for air / grasping
at straw for drawl, its phrases flopping
on the deck among the flotsam of dream.

-outsole-

breath bellies up to the bar, tending to a truth
that lures the lent ear into folklore / that stark
fathom of base reality where brash words become
the bottled worm at ink jar's black bottom and yet
still i scintillate my skull a shell-toe housing
some fillet of soul / the hull of my entire being
just a jive-ass slipper—my ideologies full of
fine bones, bass strings, and a sack o' roe . . .

-toebox-

i'm only here to take a wife; this dowry of
a deep blue sea to swaddle her swollen feet.
and don't jump forth from curtains as i sleep
or shower, trying to reel me in and scrape my scales,
demanding i surrender song in your bitters & batters
your buttermilks & other tranquilizing slurries

-heel-

you see, the circumference of my own slang
is a much better butcher's block so, please,
talk to the fish   because you don't wish
to catch the sermon in these hands.

THE FOUR CORNERS OF BECOMING WELL-ROUNDED (AS A POET)

1

everyone has a "way" of writing; do it often & it becomes your "style";
do it badly & they call it "a gimmick"; dissert your gimmick & they'll
call it "your voice." sincerity's got shit to do with it. they only want to
see you suffer, lacerated by their smiles for their approval.

2

one day you're losing sleep. the dead are passing gas in your direction;
your Black Supernal tagged by a pillaging horde as CRT. & then next
day *you gained awake,* muzzled in praise by village elders with
a cavalcade of virgins feeling your muscles; the night nuzzled
in your arms while the heavenly stars lactate a symphony.

3

but either way it's still dark. you have bags under your eyes; you still
need a bath. the new booster shot. a next payday; when not wishing for
loyalty, long life, & love you catch yourself longing for royalty checks
and the intellectual reset of a weeks-long writing retreat.

4

while taking a piss piety pays visit to the visceral black poet—
and this is why I despise The Poem: someone from an audience
approaches, their adjudicating mouth thirsty for the floral phrase,

but all *Dear Poet* did was to unfurl his esophagus, a thesaurus bookmarked by their tongue while tossing hallucinations at the audience:

“this next piece is called *filtered profile pic posing as a hologram* from my new collection, *standing ovation literary congregation blues.*”

—*BRAVA, DEAR POET, BRAH-FUCKIN'-VAH!*

(we fed doe from our palms as children, not all came back with fingers)

BAS-RELIEF 7

my vowels red grass
make dowel rod of black clouds
and trowel green sea

. . .

MEGAMORPHOSIS

July 5, 2018 @ 5:08 PM

i have no patience as a poet.
i'm even worse as a regular people.
as a person, i have no particular
chill . . . my coke spills and before
the suds settle i'm drinking 7up.

i'm on to the wok before
the kettle sucks its teeth
at the accusations of the pot.
i can't even wait for the maligning luck
after the mirror breaks,
my reflection beaming over
to the next argent surface.

i have not even the time to cast a shadow.
but i did cast a spell once: at my object
of affection who fell in love with me,
the shameful tho shimmering cur
whose aura was alive but listless.

upon waking i normalize the arrows piercing
ribcage as i tend to barren fields then feign
the end of days when mere thorns scratch my thigh.

i wooed the day. i rued
all during the night; all i had to do
was wait for love's arrival,
but teach a man to sigh and
he'll take off neighing
towards the desert.

i shatter a pinky toe
and my mouth is full of ballads
and there you have it: me staring until blind
peering straight through the sun,
eyesight glaring
through july's noon sky
seeking the soft, comforting gleam
of every twinkling star
affably ever beyond

always in a minute, never in the moment,
the radiant mood remade immediately dull
in perfect american sophistry.

BLIND NIL

to see like a poet is to have blood always in the eye;
to write as a poet is seeing the eye for the antagonist it always was.

STARDUST ONOMATOPOEIA

the tongue was made to testify
to speak when the promise comes protruding
to lay under oath with tastebuds required

a sommelier of mortal shells
distinguishing lustful contempt from
some mere, facetious contemplation

recording that infectious moment
when jarring spit becomes dulcet saliva
and our bodies above and beneath bend at will

rising obesely towards thin air
brooding before we blossom
breaking completely into *Fate*.

THE ORGAN GRINDER PAYS A BILL

come, have you? to see the phallus
dance for festered poems with cinematic
tetracycline drenching to the bone?

all your Samsung phone-bill money
misappropriated for some Phantom
of the Bojangle tickets.

like crows they flock
for the theatrical thrust
of a "Black poet's" penis vèvè

cameras a-whirl
to catch the exact moment
his sperm spoils . . .

ignored by most are his coils-of-war;
his uncouth communique
dissecting the origins of anger.

it's all about the crotch clutch on paper;
catching the stereotype begging permission
of oppression to fetch its 15 minutes.

the crime seen: a black organ dancing
to canon blast / the opera of a neon-colored
Orpheus devoid of juxtaposable juju.

“we love your spontaneous urges / it’s just
we can’t sell your Troubled Genius until
you give us guilt trip. or Black Ulysses.”

. . . .

well, now. . .
well, well, now. . .
what have we here?

HAM SAYS FUCK MY DADDY, HE CAN'T CURSE A GODDAMN THING!

how bad a fuckup are earthquakes and hurricanes
and volcanic eruptions post a physics-exempt genesis?
the corpse at the bottom of a mudslide nearly always
sides against natural selection: that fuckin' god of yours
did it! and here i am bearing witness, every single prayer
of mine swarming your senses like an airborne grudge.

*CACAO*PHONY

after

amistad came & went then the tightening
of nat turner's throat. the debates: du bois
vs. douglass

harlem's blackbeat renaissance / robert
johnson's blue jingles / mr. bojangles
templed fandango / josephine became a french
spy / jim crow & it's everlasting afterglow
the birth of cool, mingus & monk;
the death of malcolm . . .

after

came the last poets & pfunk / giovanni.
sanchez. hayden. madhubuti. all the darker
densities. the fatboys. krs. outkast.

the white man's niggers became an other color.
became black / returned to africa. philosophies
in cornbread & phosphorescence / pidgin-fire
& the pigmentation of phases / going through a phrase.

after

dark soldiers from america's kiln with their
nonconforming heat in defense of anger.
and tiredness. their scalps on fire even against
their wills

and still—*to romance.*
the softness remaining within.
the need to cherish. to have. to hold.

to seep a love to love / something supernal / always

after.

BLACK CATERPILLAR THEOREM NO. 1

a boulder is the sun
building its nest on my shoulders;
the breeze at brew in the nape of my kitchen
surrounds me in a blanket of trust.

for breakfast: coffee and cake
and this pondered plight:

    —prophecy vs. process—

to enshrine our caterpillar selves
in transcendental shine or rush, rebuilt,
as some phenomenal butterfly?

    this of course,
    is carrots vs. carts.

mustn't we master Ma'at
before metamorphism?
the stilted crawl before
any transformative hajj?
cocooning towards
some Taj Mahal, face-forward
in our own likeness?

gawk in splendid wonder
at your own auspicious genesis,
you gentle warrior before you
inch, worm, into the psychical
reconstruct where dreams
shun ground / defying
paranormal gravity
bathe in the flood
of the existentialisms within

essence expanding beyond ego
absorb all the auras of Mother
Africa made hidden

even the beetle is a beautiful thing—
protector of ants & slugs & ladybugs

know thyself, nightcrawler,
before morphing into myth
and remember:

> a butterfly is just a centipede with wings
> unable to fly to sun during rainy days
> (or other inclemental lapses) as all others.

hardships will always follow
for aches & pains have wings as well

and tho butterflies
dine on daylight it's the caterpillar
that's the most conscious;
it carries the cosmic,
not just reflects it.

above all,
it is the prism
between the limelight
& the rainbow.

so never repugn your husk
it gave you haven
as you raced for life.

WHERE FIREFLIES COME FROM

there lives a witch in Upper Ethiopia
millennia old, refuses death, not from daring,
just she done done it once or more and knows
her way around the waiting rooms of the empyreal
knows how to avoid the ephemeral rush
her heart weighed on a copper plate

you see, her pulsebeat is an aviary:
a cardiovascular system that has no fear of feathers
and flocks to faith / light as light / right as rain
always ascends.

  Legba always bends the rules for her.
  it doesn't happen often.

Hatshepsut tried jumping the velvet rope
once & found herself condemned
to the purgatory of foreigners, 5000 yrs
of punishment in their projects.

sits slumped in the first floor window
of every tenement you know, Aunt Nancy's
her nom de plume, her love song a nod to plums
holla and she'll say

"what is it, baby?
baby, what it is?"

believe me or not, it's true, I swear
on the sleeve of White Jesus
or on a slice of American cheese
(for y'all anti-ists & maybe-ists,
however y'all redefine refinement)

anyway

the Ethiopian woman, let's call her
Gladys (not her real name)—her daddy
once ruled all of Egypt with trade routes
to Tanzania: coriander & chambermaids,
juniper & concubines, a camel's weight
in cumin for a manservant
who could later run for senate or be the cowrie
shell merchant cornering the market & blazing
trails for the kola nut salesmen that followed

as a child Gladys suckled from the servant
who gave birth to a professor in Addis Ababa who
slung a secret slang to Socrates during the day
and taught Greek daughters how to get down

and do the dervish at *Thebes in the Night,* a local
hotspot; he had an MFA in astronomy, PhD
in pyramid building. his second wife learned astrology
and kept our heads on tight daydreaming of twilight

and Jim Ra was his name-o

he gave up war
and became a wise advisor but a thousand decades
into decadence later came a terroristic cloning
and Jim Ra became Jim Crow who was dead wrong
& disavowed, his unshaved head
scrubbed from every hallway in Meroë

Gladys (still not her real name)
would never succumb to inert beliefs . . .
the name change was the best way to
avert mercenaries on murderous *"missions from God."*

for a time, she also went by Ibrahima (1307–1881)
was never an imam, but her womanhood was respected.
she's lived in palaces / low rises / houses of mud / juke
jointed through Georgia while on vacation back in 1983.
rebuked the pope at the Vatican in '87 as he sat sloped
in his chair, said to him: "sit up straight; *the pharisees*
never played that shit! and your spiritual stoicism
is making my stomach hurt! plus, you really should
learn to dance . . ."
she DJ'd a house party in 1992 . . .
had a rave in a cornfield in Kentucky / laying eyes
and hands on everybody until healed. these days,
she just sits and quilts in quiet
riding a metal rocker near the 6th cataract of the Nile

sometimes tends to her gardens; a country tract
of collards and tomatoes / sewing the sun
into a grain of sand / growing temples of life
from an unforgiving land.

as of today, all of her syllables are soft
and if she just has to be harsh then she's hard halcyon
with her words. a cerulean sound that washes the blues
from your wounds and untombs you
as her obdurate song
blesses your babies.

but what's all this to do
with the genesis of fireflies?

the long fable short:

she laughs;
then they exist.

THE DISNEY+ BLACK PRINCE STORYBOARD BLUES

to die the hero as cinema
with soundtrack blaring
a black hole leaping
across the void smiling
into the camera
into the languages of light
the dawn on your shoulders
your boots full of stardust
and twilight . . . but better yet
to *not* die the hard-luck knight
the hero with a sly smile
left for dead / but instead
forever rising / many
many sequels later.

well-scripted. well-funded. & black;
the franchise of your cameo fabled.

THE LAST WILL & TESTAMENT OF A FOR REAL WOODEN BOY

after time the pixels blur / the colors slur off
the page / the dawn broken down & over the edges

the brake line of my brain is leaking / akimbo in
collapse / lungs are from timber and breath but

an ember / this simmering, lumbering life
—*my sacred phlegmnal* / true, love is stronger

than pride but not formaldehyde; my dying breath
bequeathed to love / i skint my knee and a tree

fell out its brittle bark; this seeping son of a sap
with my willows weeping a terminal flaw:

the evidence of termites down in the crawl space
of black spirit / & this is why i can't write nice poems.

SLOW WALK FROM THE EXPLODING THEME SONG

me & ike—anaconda & son
cool in cold candor, our dander up
nursery rhymes with a hard *r*
my toenail clippings will pitch yer eye out
i'm no elitist. an old man. a deletist, if anything
my blues written in blood & snot & whatnot
(or what have you)—isaac rides shotgun
my sawed-off on his lap, a juke joint in his juice box.

two old souls
we take no shit.

and if i too sucked on sippy cups it would be
full of hard jazz but i done chewed on broken
glass my entire life and now i wear dentures
capped in copper / voice is varnished.
tonsils tarnished by ruin in the throat.
a pyre-breathing houngan.

a hardened criminal & his ardent son
traveling a subliminal blue. but don't mistake
my bullshit for swashbuckle . . . my lucky talisman
is the switchblade my daddy had & mr., i'll gut you.
spells straight from the spigot / strait, no glacier.

with your lover's sleeve i brush my teeth and leave
your pot of beans bereft of onion & cornbread

i make them haints dance a hard history
but not that 400 years of old shit, known
& sandwiched between your mama's breasts
like rent money / no, not that / but wrapped
in the dance of the sunshine she sits on.
that nickel-plated obeah tucked inside a garter.
a mercurial kind of blackness / moist & throbbing.

the poems that pulse until they piss blood
i'm a bullshit shaman. a mythematist from
midway, kentucky; ike is kith & kin / our cauls
are buried in such themesongs. done sold
our souls for banjos and super sugar crisps . . .

creatures from the black legume are we.
we didn't ask to be this way but you can only
dangle real freedom in front of the emancipated for
so long before they change the song . . .
you hang a man until the bough breaks and
if his raw head & broken bones sing a redemptive
tune then that's reckoning you caint control.

IDALTUS #1 AND #2

1.

I've eaten my head—it wasn't easy.
parted locs and cut a chunk just beneath
the hairline and chewed.

ate orbital bones, cheeks, earlobes,
eardrums, medulla, pituitary, jawbone,
the tonsils.

eating one's own uvula can be messy,
and my first thought was to stop eating
at the nape, eating beyond the neck isn't necessary,
but I didn't account for *the creative process™*
being this ravenous.

I'm told this is what tenacious writers do
when faced with hypothermia—they turn
hibernation into a golden calf / slay every .pdf file
on December's golden altar,
where God's avatar is a cooling-board.

winter is embraced.

totems, hymnals, ankhs and rosary beads
are carved from glacier; vanity is sated,
the situation: still "complicated"

less tenuous.

supposedly sane,
we become groundhogs awaiting spring's
beautiful thaw; to rise up from the hallowed terrain
inside our heads, mental states ascending
from the solid earth as pearls from the clam.
every new word some opulent flora
bursting in 21st-century brightness
from the compost flaw renewed,
reenergized, emerging raw
from the soils grown old in our bodies
hoping for pollination after the bee colony collapses;
growing the monstrous from the venerable;
harvesting sunshine from our avalanches:

this is the excavation of self;
the part (for poets) where the aspects of cannibalism
catch on / where writing is as cannabis
taking us high on sentience, on algebraic sentence structure,
and self-equation.

poetry is the archeology of awkward science;
it is the removal of the oblongatas
where the mainstream has metastasized,
hatching its corporate slang
in the sealed sarcophagus that is America.

when the mummy awakes and breaks
hungrily into the open, i'm hoping he'll not find
David Livingstone taking up tenure in the cauldrons
of my folklore where the marrow of literary rejection letters
season the broth.

bucolic Africana
is more than a capable soup bone
and with my write hand I stir the pot:

bubble, bubble,
roil and rubble . . .

this is who I am.

anti-corporeal. the copper bottom
for paranormal cooking pots;
dark horse contestant on
America's next black poet™.
home-brewed, my existentialism
is endless.

this is what I do.

2.

the appendix (in its whole person)
reasserts its purpose and meets Ethiopia
in the raw where the ancestral black
body is the most buried:
the beard of the appendix is long.
songbooks are stitched into his robe, a smile
is on his face; the birthplace of stars
stain his teeth—

make no mistake
I've eaten the whole round of my head;
but what will ache next
in my appetite for reconstruction?

what black viscera will adorn my plate
for the sate of shadows?

my carnality is a cavernous thing,
and black slang is not bulimic.

the head-witch-chef-in-charge,
I've slaughtered memory and cured the hocks
of language;

yes, I've had the hunger,

I've always had
the hunger.

THE TREASURER OF THE BABALAWO GUILD DELETES HIS TWITTER ACCOUNT

—ha—

what need have I for capes, flying cars, & utility belts?
I keep a ream of lightning at all times in my 'nations sack;
a sidekick to Shango, Shiva & Jesus:
saviors all with magical negro complexes . . .

(welcome to the Ile-Ife Justice League—square pegs slotted
into a round midnight)

—ha ha—

I am secret scholar, speak the known sentence born
from living in a sentient silence / and still we are broad-day
in our everyday dialogue. we are all hardened heroes here.
devoid of mask and cowl, doing the bidding of whatever

birth cauls call for, our beautiful birthrights buried
at metaphysical intersections . . . what need we

to be vintage comic when voice was born an ancient analog?
just call and I come, your cosmic-curator curing thickened
arteries of assimilated civility, the most common brand of all
borrowed freedoms.

—ha ha ha—

understand: my power is to bore you; make you work for
what needs hearing . . . some "God for bid" need not apply.

there is radio wave in every word. in spiritwork, there is
bandwidth for everyone; spewing ashé from the mountaintop:
fountainhead for an unmapped disco-combobulation.

"conqueroos" . . . our mamas all call us "conqueroos."

GET YOUR HAND OUT OF MY POCKET

1)

the Priests of Basquiat draw reactionary vèvès
like this: first, they paint the ashen face, then
they erase the eyes, stitching Etch A Sketch
spirit beneath the breast
they replace the open mouth with communiques
from the edge of cubism; every closed word turnt
into a quadrangle, beliefs drawn and quartered
into neon and other unnatural acts of art;
an appeasement by forceful acts
this swallowing of angst: old dark men
step forth from light, reformed shysters
defending sun, living on a sustenance
of shadows—they say:

> "dare just once, youngster, to look
> like anger and they will pull your pin;
> reassemble your Rorschach and begin again,
> drenching your bone marrow in bleach;
> pick any ninny, they'll tell you
> the tongue muscle knows recombinance.
> beneath the broken myth houngans and
> double-agent mammies hide our *Collective Truths,*
> this is our double-edged-single-sided-memory. . . ."

through every porous savior / a conqueroo
is sieved; a secret service with a sankofa smile

—and if I may quote Lumumba Carson,
Loving Heart, Strong Sun, Firm Fist; We Are Those.

2)

we explode / outside in but the skin
still contains / the bent body still remains
symmetric. Olorun draws the diagram:
arrows + radii + other perforated symbols,
war paint & warning signs pointing the way

away from holocaust. we are human
implosion devices waiting for our shifts to end
for the aid of 2nd string relief workers to send
us home high, happy, hopeful . . . & hopefully healed.

down by the crossroads new-age loas
debate the nature of necessity, they contemplate
the cutting of red wires over blue. fecklessly free,
this is the length of our arrival—embracing
savant insanity as means for survival; that's
the plan of action for our bureau of counter-negligence,
contraband—renaming our secret-selves in secret . . . . . .

. . . well,
you know what they always say:

that one man's implosion is another man's—

HEY!!!

hey, nigga . . . get your hand outta my pocket!

3)

where the cameras saw a coffin
we seen a seed / all God's cosmos sealed in a casket
with Genesis drawed in the mud above it:
Olodumare doubles down on humanity.

each culture reveres its sarcophagal art,
but civilization cannot grow need from necropolis;
doing so defiles the dead and regulates them
to the role of relic, but answer this:
What race has ever survived its zombies decontextualized?

a third-eye demands a bird's-eye view;
so don't have your gods all up in my face
with their carbon-based omnipotence.

"I, too, is a God!"
so say the haints in my head.

heaven is first scrawled across the heart, crawls
and gathers composure in the mouth, enthralls us
with its wherewithals combusting—just pick

the pocket of any ninny & see if they don't up & say.

UNDOCUMENTED DENOUEMENT

i am always full of tripe
the sandstorm always at my back

and i am here to rob the bank
but always shooting blanks in my poems.

let me end from the beginning. . . .
"a t-rex steps out of a time machine," but

you've heard this one before;
i plagiarize myself; i'm a hieroglyph and

a bubblegum wrapper—a photoshopped
free verse stuck to the bottom of a cheap sneaker

anyway, i hate it when i wake up humming . . .
the sonogram sung in my sleep, its silhouette safe

and snug; this poem *(purchased like a drug*
at the slug saloon) casts a preemptive shadow

my hand in your ass-pocket for your wallet
and lingering too long in the hand of your wife

because i'm tripe. and bullshit;
just the two . . .

and jazz . . . and funk . . .
and hip hop . . . *and the blue!*

(what's a little black lie between
App friends forced to facebook?)

whistling at the white women
at the black lives matter rally . . .

and so unprecedential at the podium delivering
my state of the snafu address / sorry,

but i'm not sneakin' any second term
i was born on january 21st, not the 6th . . .

and if you change the channel i'll smite you!
too late, i've already smited. you've been smoted.

or smooted? in the very least, i done already
pooted in your direction.

hallelujah, allahu akbar, jumpin' jehosaphat,
nam-myoho-renge-kyo / a pocket full of posies,

ashes / ashes . . . aché anshit . . . *praxis? we talkin'*
about praxis?!   ¯_(´´/)_/¯

—you know how the bit go—and i think
i've left the water running; although, somewhere,

there's always a water running / i'm the son of a
drought and this wail's run dry—my grimace stout

no pinnace envy;
two tears in a bucket / trebuchet

half man;
half a muezzin.

FEARING TO ANALOG ON THE GROUNDS HE MIGHT DISCRIMINATE HIMSELF THE BLACK DIGITAL POET PLEADS "*DA FIF*"—BUT IS HE ALREADY TOO LATE?

(aka, a literary mob boss offers mama a house in exchange for my silence)

a prosecutor addresses the literary judges:

we suffer from
a dysmorphophobic dialogue syndrome
forcing enjambment
into suits and ties behind sword and shield
our disinvested voices
overdressed in licorice stick and mock turtlenecks
our butterfly collars
have become a closed caption shackled
within our steam trunks
held down at the footboards of our brass beds
every phrase a notion
within a notion; footnotes on the ass end of fairy tale
foaming over like a fast-food latte

the end result is a rhythmless Rorschach;
similes for a cement boot . . . where's the beef?
no, my brother, where's the goddamn beat street!

exhibits are presented to the jury:

there's little grant money
in the branch-diluvian writers guild for broken obsidian,
for pedagogies like this one, with psychosis unaffiliated

to eat right, we'll awake—wince and famous, as seen on tv;
the ghost head of Langston Hughes floating above our beds,
his gift horse weeping onto our pillows as pageantries on page
smile down at us from bookshelves and mantels, every script
a trophy for the language of lycanthropes.

if only our slingshots and shotguns came ready-loaded
with quicksilver; make each of us a slayer of distended
symphonies... but where ours was once a pretty pidgin,
our written words are now single bodied like amoebae,
a monosyllabic hemoglobin.

the poet on trial takes the stand and offers rebuttal:

where's my lawyer? I wanna address the jury...
lies / it's all lies! this whole court is in contempt / you
motherfuckers caint handle the— wait...
is that a camera?

are we on cable?
why, yes, I am able / I am willing / definitely I am willing,
all my words are polished lit's plush alibi
my gentrified testimony is ready for totems and urns
and temples atop ol' hallowed Mt. Olympussy
and them other limp literary perjuries
paved in photoshop:

o' what a trend we have in symmetry;
oh, precious blurb, come take my hand!

an insular jury rolls its eyes; the sketch artist coughs
into his sleeve; the small publisher goes into witness protection;
the reality tv producer rescinds a contract.

the poet on trial drops a dime & cops a plea:

what's that, Mr. Prosecutor? you mean that poet-professor
with the patch-eye & scar for a smile? why I've never seent
that man before in my life! for all I know, that crooked letter
is a clean man . . . something like a Samaritan,
to let the liquor tell it.

why didn't he just yesterday reinvent for us *the paragon?*

but, yes, I seent the whole thing unfurl . . .

(he points & he stands)
and if I was gwan pin the whole rap
on some gullible schmuck *then that therre golem did it!*
husslin' yodels for publishin' deals and caramel lattes

off of 7th & lime. don't he
juss look the loser?!?

exhibit m:

the poet on trial on surveillance cam
"buying" tired poems & used Ghazals at gunpoint
from a pawnshop in Little Africa; behind him
a white hood with a patch-eye and scarred smile
pressing his jacket pocket into the poet's back. . . .

solemn, the judge unfolds a napkin before him
hiding pencil shavings & several small knuckles,
"OH, NO!"
the presiding juror falls back aghast and gray . . .
the poet on trial—rolls his eyes and looks away,
whistlin' dixie against his will. . . .

psalm of the defense counsel:
sing, o friend, your lubricious lit
you two-faced, double-dealing, code-switching sneak.
flap your oblique gums in cold critique, dry-snitching,
thumbing your nose / your prose thrumming.
who knew your smile could be so guileful?

"meanwhile . . ."
in the corner of each poem's comic panel; your flannel
language is out to fleece . . . well, "fuck the police"
"and their little dog, too" with Mr. Magoo
as the predator-in-chief of every literary journal
with little belief in works submitted.

what a sin; what a shame . . .

"and if you ask me again, I'll t-tell you the same."

closing arguments (aka ballad of the hung jury):

> *"Bum stiggedy bum stiggedy bum, hon,*
> *I got the old pa-rum-pum-pum-pum"*

aside of the bail bondsman:

> we were last seen hunting minotaurs
> on a grecian urn—a prophecy in clay
> kilned millennia ago in what is present-day DRC.
> but eons later, *"I caint take you nowhair!"* became
> the clarion call passed from ashen'd lap to perched ass
> on the playgrounds of America's Southern Black Belt,
> and now all the system-bred poets are all cursed,
> degreed, and speak a condensed, dissing spell.

the defense attorney covers the mic to speak into the ear of his client:

> well, Fey Prince, you had your fun,
> but we no longer reek for you.
>
> as before, we hunt our own meats:
>   medusa-head stew; prime rib of centaur;
>   aesop au gratin; pegasus chichinga...
> each an untamed chitlin brought to heel.
>
>   have you never been
>   to the bush of ghosts?!?

well, no wonder the befuddlement! (knee slap!)
there's a reason the European unicorn's been hunted
to extinction, just as lynch mobs sought
the oyster meats of Africa, the game afoot
the hunt, as they say, *has always been afoot!*

asides of the likely condemned man's mother, hair rollers collapsing:

lay down, Little Prince, with your head
the Prime Meridian for Dr. Seuss, you cruel,
cruel *Cristofer Roben*, tiny depressed king
of your very own Camelot . . . I, as well, was a child
but had grown to envy your baubles, and parables,
and the privileges you would inherit . . .

aside:
life is never kind, child-king, and I know that you,
too, have spilled your milk, scraped a knee, been forced
to eat brussels before cookies and
pudding. we all have cried over childish concerns—a
precocious concerto—wanting cake for breakfast,
having to settle for an under-buttered batter of gruel.
how pitiful our impish little, pitter-patter sounded
and made to suffer, like Poor Max—off to bed without
supper; what disloyalty to a Wild Thing Royal having
his impending sovereignty savagely ignored . . . or take
Poor Little Sambo, so Brave (when not being Black) tho
never seen as spirited or spry or even fey, which was so
unfair . . . taught to avoid adventure; that trouble, child,
would come to him like a Grimm thing hungry for his
flesh, his songs, and for his sense of fashion.

aside, aside:

what a contemporary fairytale / this theatrics
in three rings: 1. the jumping down, 2. the turning
around, 3. the picking bales of cotton; this heirloom
yeast kneading our stories, feasting on the collective
like a Midway Mortician famished for the deeds
ceded to bereaving widows and their pallbearing
brood. remember how the tobacco-leaf-bellied
people all took advantage? *"a pine box"* they said, *"for
your 41 acres, your 2 mules."*

a tale as old as crime.

the poet on trial prays to higher powers:

O Holy Force-Fed Fairytales of Foreigners:
forgive me in this suborned moment.

how foolish I now sound, how unreasonably jealous;
complaining of this culture-in-the-round gifted to us by
those whose only favorite joy was to keep us in the dark,
worshipping a luster we could neither question or modify

and we've ruined it, preserving petulance
in the ambers of our own niggardly syntax.

I s'pose that ol' negro proverb, it seems, is true:

you really can't take us anywhere.

to everyone's surprise, the poet on trial is acquitted
(ode to a clean slate):

yeah, now what!
I told you fuckers I didn't do it! (and y'all believed me?!)
what even was the charges?!?
• 27 counts possession of unlicensed free verse
    w/ intent to internet
• 33 counts of pen-handling
• 6 counts soliciting unsafe text within 500 feet
    of a small press.
• 3 counts possession of a bookbinding stapler and
    several reams of newsprint with intent to chapbook
• gobs and gobs counts of journaling while nonacademic
    outside a pre-assigned genre.
• 755 counts of doodling in book margins.

Well . . . yeah. yeah. I did that—but goddamn—

y'all almost got me! / "double indemnity," amirite?

that was close. y'all so suck at this . . .
ha, haaa! but fareal tho . . . fareal, fareal . . .
it's no mean feat, no soft miracle,
being an uncredentialed poet
with no professional YouTube
and hardly 300 followers in 5 years of Instagram;
no graduating MFA class to exchange photobombs,
no artsy literary collective to disband with
once fame is gained and jealousy dampens

I've worn, in farinaceous dreams,
the mammoth's severed head & the centaur's
iridescent bottom, hunting African Ovids in Autumn
avoiding Narcissus & Invidia and the Vestal Virgins
where the safe trend is to CGI Circe in nacreous rhyme,
to place her in a Cubs cap (after nightclub) at
the Waffle House, the Whore House, the White House's bomb
   shelter . . .
but i'm never one to linger on the likes
of Hera or the love life of Amphitrite nor on Antheia's
green thumb . . . I'm rooted in an invisible missive,
a magnetic juju / behind this palisade of constellations,
this Inzalo Y'Langa, I am most at home
reclaiming my divinity in this birthplace of the sun.

in this birthplace of the sun, I remain a gardener of ghosts.

BAS-RELIEF 8

your entire sun sunken
your evening trashed & thrashing
lured here & floundering in immortal pleonasm:

a *goobledygook*   a *bafflegab* . . .

a "mess-o'-pieces theater"

a complete baste of time

"the black poet wrote a tsunami," you snark
"and here we are without a snorkel!"

your undivided attention   *drowning* in prolixity
in close proximity to complete damnation

'til finally: you're up for air and you wonder if you're woke

and it dawns on you "i'm never getting back this hour."
(i warned you at the start i was pablum of sun & you laughed)

another garrulous poet.

"see, this is why i hate coming out to readings!"

—but i thank you, patron, for your devotion. your patience.

—after questions there'll be a signing.
(maybe drinks & dining for the inner circle)

. . .

so,   like & subscribe   please—*if you could*
and—*if you would*—please remain on hold for a brief survey.